HAL•LEONARD
INSTRUMENTAL
PLAY-ALONG

AUDIO
ACCESS
INCLUDED

PLAYBACK+
Speed • Pitch • Balance • Loop

ALTO SAX

JAZZ CLASSICS

T0068869

Audio arrangements by Peter Deneff

To access audio visit:
www.halleonard.com/mylibrary

Enter Code
6624-8441-5494-6054

ISBN 978-1-4950-4749-7

HAL•LEONARD®
7777 W. BLUEMOUND RD. P.O. BOX 13819 MILWAUKEE, WI 53213

For all works contained herein:
Unauthorized copying, arranging, adapting, recording, Internet posting, public performance,
or other distribution of the printed or recorded music in this publication is an infringement of copyright.
Infringers are liable under the law.

Visit Hal Leonard Online at
www.halleonard.com

DOXY

ALTO SAX

By SONNY ROLLINS

Copyright © 1963 Prestige Music c/o The Bicycle Music Company
Copyright Renewed
International Copyright Secured   All Rights Reserved

IN WALKED BUD

ALTO SAX

By THELONIOUS MONK

Copyright © 1948 (Renewed) by Embassy Music Corporation (BMI)
International Copyright Secured   All Rights Reserved
Reprinted by Permission

IN YOUR OWN SWEET WAY

ALTO SAX

By DAVE BRUBECK

Copyright © 1955, 1956 by Derry Music Co.
Copyright Renewed
Sole Selling Agent: Shawnee Press, Inc.
International Copyright Secured   All Rights Reserved
Reprinted by Permission

MERCY, MERCY, MERCY

ALTO SAX

Composed by JOSEF ZAWINUL

Copyright © 1966 Zawinul Enterprises LLC
Copyright Renewed
All Rights Administered by Songs Of Kobalt Music Publishing
All Rights Reserved   Used by Permission

NARDIS

ALTO SAX

By MILES DAVIS

Copyright © 1959 Jazz Horn Music Corporation
Copyright Renewed
All Rights Administered by Songs Of Kobalt Music Publishing
All Rights Reserved   Used by Permission

ON GREEN DOLPHIN STREET

ALTO SAX

Lyrics by NED WASHINGTON
Music by BRONISLAU KAPER

© 1947 (Renewed) Catharine Hinen Music, Patti Washington Music and Primary Wave Songs
All Rights for Catharine Hinen Music Controlled by Shapiro, Bernstein & Co., Inc.
All Rights for Primary Wave Songs Controlled by EMI April Music Inc. (Publishing) and Alfred Music (Print)
All Rights Reserved   Used by Permission

REUNION BLUES

ALTO SAX

By MILT JACKSON

Copyright © 1962 (Renewed 1990) by MJQ Music, Inc.
All Rights Administered by Hal Leonard - Milwin Music Corp.
International Copyright Secured   All Rights Reserved

STOLEN MOMENTS

ALTO SAX

Words and Music by
OLIVER NELSON

Copyright © 1962, 1965 by Noslen Music Co. LLC
Copyright Renewed
All Rights for the World Administered by Alameda Music Company
International Copyright Secured   All Rights Reserved
Used by Permission

ST. THOMAS

ALTO SAX

By SONNY ROLLINS

Copyright © 1963 Prestige Music c/o The Bicycle Music Company
Copyright Renewed
International Copyright Secured   All Rights Reserved

SCRAPPLE FROM THE APPLE

ALTO SAX

By CHARLIE PARKER

Copyright © 1957 (Renewed 1985) Atlantic Music Corp.
International Copyright Secured   All Rights Reserved

SIDEWINDER

ALTO SAX

By Lee MORGAN

Copyright © 1959 (Renewed) Conrad Music (BMI)
U.S. Rights owned by Arc/Conrad Music LLC (Administered by BMG Rights Management (US) LLC)
International Copyright Secured   All Rights Reserved

TAKE FIVE

ALTO SAX

By PAUL DESMOND

© 1960 (Renewed 1988) Desmond Music Company
All Rights outside the USA Controlled by Derry Music Company
International Copyright Secured   All Rights Reserved

HAL•LEONARD INSTRUMENTAL PLAY-ALONG

Your favorite songs are arranged just for solo instrumentalists with this outstanding series. Each book includes a great full-accompaniment play-along audio so you can sound just like a pro! Check out **www.halleonard.com** to see all the titles available.

The Beatles

All You Need Is Love • Blackbird • Day Tripper • Eleanor Rigby • Get Back • Here, There and Everywhere • Hey Jude • I Will • Let It Be • Lucy in the Sky with Diamonds • Ob-La-Di, Ob-La-Da • Penny Lane • Something • Ticket to Ride • Yesterday.

_____ 00225330	Flute	$14.99
_____ 00225331	Clarinet	$14.99
_____ 00225332	Alto Sax	$14.99
_____ 00225333	Tenor Sax	$14.99
_____ 00225334	Trumpet	$14.99
_____ 00225335	Horn	$14.99
_____ 00225336	Trombone	$14.99
_____ 00225337	Violin	$14.99
_____ 00225338	Viola	$14.99
_____ 00225339	Cello	$14.99

Chart Hits

All About That Bass • All of Me • Happy • Radioactive • Roar • Say Something • Shake It Off • A Sky Full of Stars • Someone like You • Stay with Me • Thinking Out Loud • Uptown Funk.

_____ 00146207	Flute	$12.99
_____ 00146208	Clarinet	$12.99
_____ 00146209	Alto Sax	$12.99
_____ 00146210	Tenor Sax	$12.99
_____ 00146211	Trumpet	$12.99
_____ 00146212	Horn	$12.99
_____ 00146213	Trombone	$12.99
_____ 00146214	Violin	$12.99
_____ 00146215	Viola	$12.99
_____ 00146216	Cello	$12.99

Coldplay

Clocks • Every Teardrop Is a Waterfall • Fix You • In My Place • Lost! • Paradise • The Scientist • Speed of Sound • Trouble • Violet Hill • Viva La Vida • Yellow.

_____ 00103337	Flute	$12.99
_____ 00103338	Clarinet	$12.99
_____ 00103339	Alto Sax	$12.99
_____ 00103340	Tenor Sax	$12.99
_____ 00103341	Trumpet	$12.99
_____ 00103342	Horn	$12.99
_____ 00103343	Trombone	$12.99
_____ 00103344	Violin	$12.99
_____ 00103345	Viola	$12.99
_____ 00103346	Cello	$12.99

Disney Greats

Arabian Nights • Hawaiian Roller Coaster Ride • It's a Small World • Look Through My Eyes • Yo Ho (A Pirate's Life for Me) • and more.

_____ 00841934	Flute	$12.99
_____ 00841935	Clarinet	$12.99
_____ 00841936	Alto Sax	$12.99
_____ 00841937	Tenor Sax	$12.95
_____ 00841938	Trumpet	$12.99
_____ 00841939	Horn	$12.99
_____ 00841940	Trombone	$12.95
_____ 00841941	Violin	$12.99
_____ 00841942	Viola	$12.99
_____ 00841943	Cello	$12.99
_____ 00842078	Oboe	$12.99

Great Themes

Bella's Lullaby • Chariots of Fire • Get Smart • Hawaii Five-O Theme • I Love Lucy • The Odd Couple • Spanish Flea • and more.

_____ 00842468	Flute	$12.99
_____ 00842469	Clarinet	$12.99
_____ 00842470	Alto Sax	$12.99
_____ 00842471	Tenor Sax	$12.99
_____ 00842472	Trumpet	$12.99
_____ 00842473	Horn	$12.99
_____ 00842474	Trombone	$12.99
_____ 00842475	Violin	$12.99
_____ 00842476	Viola	$12.99
_____ 00842477	Cello	$12.99

Popular Hits

Breakeven • Fireflies • Halo • Hey, Soul Sister • I Gotta Feeling • I'm Yours • Need You Now • Poker Face • Viva La Vida • You Belong with Me • and more.

_____ 00842511	Flute	$12.99
_____ 00842512	Clarinet	$12.99
_____ 00842513	Alto Sax	$12.99
_____ 00842514	Tenor Sax	$12.99
_____ 00842515	Trumpet	$12.99
_____ 00842516	Horn	$12.99
_____ 00842517	Trombone	$12.99
_____ 00842518	Violin	$12.99
_____ 00842519	Viola	$12.99
_____ 00842520	Cello	$12.99

Songs from Frozen, Tangled and Enchanted

Do You Want to Build a Snowman? • For the First Time in Forever • Happy Working Song • I See the Light • In Summer • Let It Go • Mother Knows Best • That's How You Know • True Love's First Kiss • When Will My Life Begin • and more.

_____ 00126921	Flute	$14.99
_____ 00126922	Clarinet	$14.99
_____ 00126923	Alto Sax	$14.99
_____ 00126924	Tenor Sax	$14.99
_____ 00126925	Trumpet	$14.99
_____ 00126926	Horn	$14.99
_____ 00126927	Trombone	$14.99
_____ 00126928	Violin	$14.99
_____ 00126929	Viola	$14.99
_____ 00126930	Cello	$14.99

Top Hits

Adventure of a Lifetime • Budapest • Die a Happy Man • Ex's & Oh's • Fight Song • Hello • Let It Go • Love Yourself • One Call Away • Pillowtalk • Stitches • Writing's on the Wall.

_____ 00171073	Flute	$12.99
_____ 00171074	Clarinet	$12.99
_____ 00171075	Alto Sax	$12.99
_____ 00171106	Tenor Sax	$12.99
_____ 00171107	Trumpet	$12.99
_____ 00171108	Horn	$12.99
_____ 00171109	Trombone	$12.99
_____ 00171110	Violin	$12.99
_____ 00171111	Viola	$12.99
_____ 00171112	Cello	$12.99

Wicked

As Long As You're Mine • Dancing Through Life • Defying Gravity • For Good • I'm Not That Girl • Popular • The Wizard and I • and more.

_____ 00842236	Flute	$12.99
_____ 00842237	Clarinet	$12.99
_____ 00842238	Alto Saxophone	$11.95
_____ 00842239	Tenor Saxophone	$11.95
_____ 00842240	Trumpet	$11.99
_____ 00842241	Horn	$11.95
_____ 00842242	Trombone	$12.99
_____ 00842243	Violin	$11.99
_____ 00842244	Viola	$12.99
_____ 00842245	Cello	$12.99

Prices, contents, and availability subject to change without notice.
Disney characters and artwork © Disney Enterprises, Inc.